OCTOBER

Ellen Jackson

Illustrated by
Robin DeWitt and Pat DeWitt

ini Charlesbridge

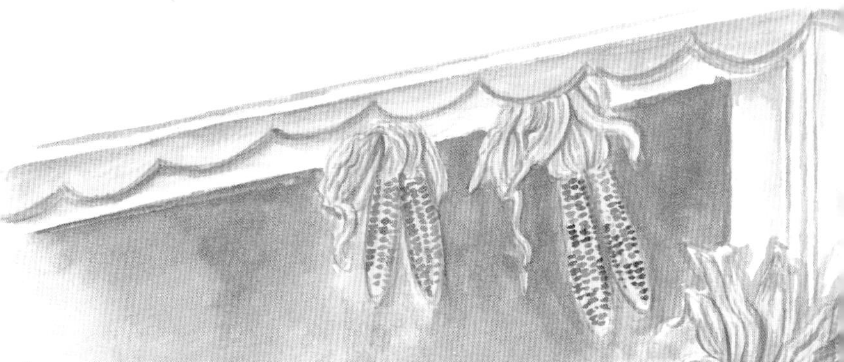

To my dear friend Kathy Wilson Crook—E. J.

To our mother and father,
Stella and Gilbert DeWitt.
Thanks for giving us life and
everything that makes it worth living.
—R. D. & P. D.

Did You Know?

October is a month of mystery. On windy nights, doors creak, windows rattle, and owls hoot in the darkness.

Early in the month, the symbols of Halloween start to appear—black cats, ghosts, and goblins. Large, orange pumpkins are heaped in piles at roadside stands ready to be made into jack-o'-lanterns and pumpkin pie.

By the end of October, most of the songbirds have gone south for the winter. One North American bird, the bobolink, passes through the Caribbean during this time of year. For this reason, the people of the West Indies call it the October bird.

Two animals that hunt at night, bats and owls, are also symbols of October. There are a lot of superstitions about them both, but many of these beliefs are not true. Bats are not dirty or blind, and they will not get in your hair. Owls are not blind during the day although they do see much better after dark. Their huge, staring eyes may have helped create the legend of the "wise old owl," but owls are no wiser than any other bird.

People are busy with outdoor activities during October. The crisp, cool days are just right for roaming through the woods to collect leaves or search for empty birds' nests. An American poet, Paul Laurence Dunbar, wrote that October "decks herself in garments bold / Of scarlet, purple, red, and gold."

October is also an indoor month. It is a time to build a fire in the fireplace, tell a spooky story, or watch the World Series on television. The baseball season is almost over, but the ice hockey season is just beginning.

A cold October evening is a great time for an indoor sport such as bowling. Bowling is a simple game that anyone can play. It is also an ancient game. Objects that look like bowling pins and balls were found buried with an Egyptian boy who died more than seven thousand years ago. Bocce, a game similar to bowling, was played by Roman soldiers more than two thousand years ago and remains popular in Italy today.

Field hockey, another sport often played in the
fall, is thought to be one of the first stick-and-ball
games. Games similar to hockey were played by the
ancient Greeks, Romans, and Arabs. Today girls and
boys all over the world play field hockey.

The October Birthstone

The birthstone for October is the opal. Opals
have a special, fiery glow, and they gleam with
many brilliant colors. Long ago, people in some
parts of Europe believed that opals could make
their owners invisible. For this reason, these gems
were sometimes called thief stones. A particularly
beautiful red opal was owned by the empress
Josephine, wife of Napoleon, emperor of France.

The October Flower

If you were born in October, your special flower is
the dahlia. The dahlia is native to Central America
and was brought to Europe by Spanish explorers.
This beautiful red flower was sacred to the Aztecs,
who called it the war flower. According to a legend,
Huitzilopochtli, the Aztec war god, was born fully
grown from a dahlia petal pierced by a maguey leaf.

The October Zodiac

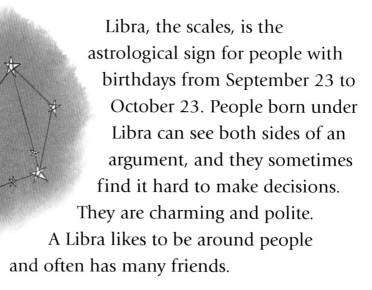

Libra, the scales, is the
astrological sign for people with
birthdays from September 23 to
October 23. People born under
Libra can see both sides of an
argument, and they sometimes
find it hard to make decisions.
They are charming and polite.
A Libra likes to be around people
and often has many friends.

The sign for people born from October 24
to November 21 is Scorpio, the scorpion.
Those born under Scorpio are said to
like puzzles of all kinds, and they
make great detectives. They love
Halloween, monster stories,
and mysteries, and they can
usually get what they want.
A Scorpio is thought
to be brave but can
also be stubborn.

The Calendar

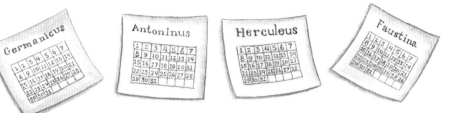

October is the tenth month of the year and has thirty-one days. In ancient Rome, the year began in March, not January. October was then the eighth month, and its name comes from the Latin word *octo*, which means "eight."

Roman leaders were not happy that some of the months were named for numbers and not for people. They tried to rename October, calling it at various times *Germanicus, Antoninus,* and *Herculeus.* For a while, October was named after a woman, Faustina, wife of Antoninus. But none of these names lasted long, and the month continued to be called October.

Sun, Sky, and Weather

In October, the days are mostly mild. Twilight comes early in the Northern Hemisphere, bringing the faint tang of burning leaves. The stars have a frosty glitter, and the nights are nippy.

The constellation Ursa Major, which means "Great Bear" in Latin, is near the horizon in the northern sky. A legend says that in the autumn, the Great Bear washes her paws in the northern lakes just before the lakes become covered by winter ice.

On the prairie, the morning is sunny, but by noon, dark clouds appear on the horizon. Hot and cold air mix and swirl upward into big, black thunderheads, and bolts of lightning flash from the sky. An American folk saying describes October weather: "There is no usual weather on the prairie. It is all unusual."

October has had many names. The Anglo-Saxons, who settled in Britain in the fifth and sixth centuries, called October *Win monath* because it was the month when wine was made and *Winterfylleth,* "winter falls," because they considered October the beginning of winter. The October full moon is sometimes called the hunter's moon because hunting season starts at this time.

Animals in October

Canada geese fly south, making a graceful V in the sky. Brook trout swim upstream to lay their eggs, and monarch butterflies from the eastern half of the United States fly thousands of miles to reach their winter home in Mexico. In the autumn, snow begins to fall in the mountains, and deer move down to the valleys, where grass can still be found.

Some animals stay in the north and prepare themselves for the cold winter ahead. Honeybees use sticky sap from buds and trees to seal cracks in their hives. Chipmunks line their nests with thistledown, and muskrats clean out their burrows and make new entrances.

October is mating season for many mammals. Porcupines waddle through the woods, sniffing as they go. These animals have poor eyesight, but they can smell the fruity, pineapple odor of another porcupine. When a male and female meet, they court each other with yowls and wails.

Male elk, called bucks, now have a full set of antlers and are ready to fight for a female. If two bucks meet, they clash horns in head-to-head combat. Usually the smaller male will run away after a brief battle, and neither elk will get hurt.

October is also mating season for pronghorn antelope on the Great Plains. Males fight with one another or charge imaginary enemies. Pronghorns, sometimes called prairie ghosts, can reach a speed of sixty miles an hour, easily outrunning any animals that try to catch them.

In the desert, the lazuli bunting is passing through on its way to Mexico, where it will spend the winter. The lazuli bunting has a sturdy bill for cracking seeds. Temperatures are still high in the desert, and this tiny bird must search for water in order to survive.

In the suburbs, skunks are looking for food and a warm place to sleep for the winter. They are attracted to garbage cans or bowls of pet food, and they often burrow under houses or barns. Skunks eat almost anything, including grasshoppers, bees, spiders, snakes, bird eggs, berries, nuts, and frogs. Some experts believe the city of Chicago got its name from an Ojibwa word that means "place of the skunk."

Plants in October

In the woods, beechnuts, butternuts, and hazelnuts have ripened, and acorns are dropping from the oaks. Milkweed pods release their seeds, which float away on silky parachutes.

Most of the wildflowers are gone now, but the trees are ablaze with color. The elms and birches are yellow. The sugar maples are red or gold with a blush of pink. Oak leaves turn scarlet, then burgundy, then brown.

Have you ever wondered why leaves change color in the fall? During the spring and summer, most leaves contain chlorophyll, the green chemical that helps make food for the trees. Other colors are also present in the leaves, but they are hidden by the bright green chlorophyll. In the winter, the trees rest and live off the food they have stored during the summer. They stop making chlorophyll, the green fades, and fall colors appear.

Fall colors also paint the prairie. Big bluestem, little bluestem, and prairie dropseed turn beautiful shades of bronze and gold as winter approaches.

Special Days

Columbus Day

On October 12, 1492, three small sailing ships carrying Christopher Columbus and his crew reached an island off the coast of North America. Columbus was not looking for the Americas. He was looking for a new way to get to Asia. He thought that he had reached Japan or China, and he continued to believe that for the rest of his life.

Historians think that Columbus landed on one of the small islands of the Bahamas. While some experts believe that Columbus was not the first European to reach the Americas, there is no doubt that his voyage changed world history. Because of Columbus's voyage, a new continent was opened to European exploration and settlement.

Today Columbus Day is a national holiday in the United States and is observed on the second Monday in October.

Halloween

Long ago, ancient people believed that ghosts and witches wandered the earth in late October. In the eighth century, November 1 became All Hallows Day, a day to honor the saints. But many people still thought that ghosts walked the earth on All Hallows Eve, October 31. Later, the name *All Hallows Eve* was shortened to *Halloween*.

An old Irish legend tells of a man named Jack who was too mean to go to heaven and who had played too many tricks on the devil to go to hell. When Jack died, he was forced to walk the earth carrying a hollow turnip with a burning ember inside. From this legend came the Irish practice of placing jack-o'-lanterns in windows.

In Ireland, Scotland, and Great Britain, candles and lanterns were lit to keep spirits away on Halloween. When people went outside, they wore costumes or masks to scare off ghosts and witches.

When many immigrants came to North America in the 1800s, Halloween customs began to be observed in the United States and Canada, too. Today children dress up as monsters, fairies, or ghosts and scare their friends or go to Halloween parties. Haunted houses, spooky movies, popcorn, and candy are part of the fun.

Famous October Events

In 1964, October 9 was named Leif Eriksson Day by President Lyndon Johnson. Native Americans had inhabited the American continents for thousands of years, but Leif Eriksson, a Norwegian explorer, is thought to have been one of the first Europeans to visit North America. Many historians believe that Leif Eriksson landed in Nova Scotia or Newfoundland between A.D. 1000 and 1003.

In 1582, the month of October had only twenty-one days! Pope Gregory XIII decided that the day following Tuesday, October 4, 1582, would actually be Friday, October 15, 1582. Pope Gregory did this because the Julian calendar was not accurate. Most Catholic countries adopted the new calendar right away, but Great Britain and the American colonies used the old calendar until 1752.

On October 8, 1871, two disastrous fires occurred. Driven by a strong wind, a fire destroyed about one third of Chicago, Illinois. The fire burned 17,450 buildings and left 250 people dead. In Wisconsin on the same day, a fire destroyed farms and settlements over a 2,400-square-mile area and swept through the town of Peshtigo, killing over 600 people.

On October 31, 1941, a famous monument honoring four great American presidents was completed. The Mount Rushmore National Memorial, located in the Black Hills of South Dakota, displays the heads of George Washington, Thomas Jefferson, Theodore Roosevelt, and Abraham Lincoln carved in stone. Each head is approximately sixty feet high.

Birthdays

Many famous people were born in October.

Thirty-ninth president of the United States, who helped create an important peace treaty between Egypt and Israel.

Indian leader who freed his country from British rule using nonviolent methods.

Architect and artist, best known for her design of the United States Vietnam Veterans Memorial.

Civil-rights leader and candidate for president in 1984 and 1988.

John Lennon

October 9, 1940

British singer, songwriter, and member of the Beatles.

Eleanor Roosevelt

October 11, 1884

Writer, humanitarian, and wife of President Franklin Delano Roosevelt.

Dwight D. Eisenhower

October 14, 1890

Thirty-fourth president of the United States and commander of the Allies in Europe during World War II.

Mae C. Jemison

October 17, 1956

Physician and the world's first female African American astronaut to enter space.

Edson Arantes do Nascimento

October 23, 1940

Better known as Pelé. World-famous Brazilian soccer player.

Theodore Roosevelt

October 27, 1858

Cowboy, explorer, author, soldier, and twenty-sixth president of the United States.

An October Folktale

A cheerful old woman was walking through the
woods on Halloween when she came upon a black
pot lying in the path. The old woman glanced inside.

"Mercy!" she said. "It's filled with gold pieces!"

The sun was going down, and an owl screeched in
a nearby tree. The old woman gathered up the pot
and hurried toward home thinking of all the good
things she could buy with the gold. But when she
glanced in the pot again, it was filled with silver!

"Well, well, I was sure it was gold," she thought.
"But who needs riches? Silver will pay the rent."

On she walked with the wind whistling in the trees. Soon her curiosity got the upper hand, and she glanced in the pot again. This time it was filled with copper.

"My old eyes are playing tricks tonight," she thought. "But these pennies will buy me a new bonnet. Won't that be grand!"

So on she walked, until once more, she glanced in the pot. This time, it was empty! Suddenly the pot gave a shriek, and two webbed wings sprouted from its sides. Then it fluttered off into the trees!

"That's a very strange pot," thought the old woman, who always looked on the bright side. "Good riddance, I say. And who needs an old pot? I have the best thing of all now—a Halloween story to tell my grandson!"

And on she walked, whistling a merry tune.

AUTHOR'S NOTE

This book gives an overview of the month of October. But nature does not follow a strict schedule. The mating and migration of animals, the blooming of plants, and other natural events vary from year to year, or occur earlier or later in different places.

The zodiac sections of this book are included just for fun as part of the folklore of the month and should not be taken as accurate descriptions of any real people.

The Halloween tale was adapted from "The Hedley Kow" by Joseph Jacobs from *Ghosts* edited by William Mayne. (New York: Thomas Nelson Inc., 1971.)

Text copyright © 2002 by Ellen Jackson
Illustrations copyright © 2002
  by Robin DeWitt and Pat DeWitt
All rights reserved, including the right of
  reproduction in whole or in part in any form.

Published by Charlesbridge Publishing
85 Main Street, Watertown, MA 02472
(617) 926-0329
www.charlesbridge.com

Illustrations done in watercolor on Arches
  hot-press paper
Display type and text type set in Giovanni
Color separations made by Sung In Printing,
  South Korea
Printed and bound by Sung In Printing,
  South Korea
Production supervision by Brian G. Walker
Designed by Diane M. Earley

**Library of Congress
Cataloging-in-Publication Data**

Jackson, Ellen B., 1943-
    October/Ellen Jackson; illustrated by
    Robin DeWitt and Pat DeWitt.
      p.cm.—(It happens in the month of)
    ISBN 0-88106-923-X (hardcover)
    1. October—Folklore. 2. October—Juvenile
literature. [1. October.] I. DeWitt, Robin,
ill. II. DeWitt, Pat, ill. III. Title.

GR930.J342   2002
398'.33—dc21   2001023508

Printed in South Korea
10 9 8 7 6 5 4 3 2 1